NEW JERSEY

A Photographic Treasure

Dedicated
with love to my treasures,
Susan and Joe

NEW JERSEY

A Photographic Treasure

WALTER CHOROSZEWSKI

Published by

AESTHETIC PRESS, INC.

SOMERVILLE, NEW JERSEY

NEW JERSEY, *A Photographic Treasure*

© 2002 Aesthetic Press, Inc., All Rights Reserved
All Photography © 2002 Walter Choroszewski, All Rights Reserved
Edited and designed by Walter Choroszewski
Printed in Korea - Second Printing 2003

ISBN 0-933605-13-7

AESTHETIC PRESS, INC.
PO Box 5306, Somerville, NJ 08876-1303

www.aestheticpress.com
email: info@aestheticpress.com
Telephone: 908 369-3777

Cover
Worthington State Forest,
Warren County

Half Title
High Point State Park,
Sussex County

Treasures

by

Walter Choroszewski

I feel blessed when I see the kaleidoscope of colors found in an Atlantic Ocean sunrise, or the almost iridescent glow of moss-covered rocks along a Kittatinny Mountain stream, or the star-like twinkle of the Outerbridge lights reflecting in the Arthur Kill below. I am rich from these experiences.

Wealth, accumulated or stored; ... a collection of precious things. These words define "treasure" and they most aptly describe New Jersey. The word "treasure" also shares a common origin with the word "thesaurus" ...a storehouse or treasury of words or information, interrelated and cross-referenced. Again, New Jersey comes to mind with its abundant natural beauty, rich history and mosaic of people—all entwined within a compact, yet varied, landscape stretching from mountains to sea.

For more than twenty years I have been fortunate to discover and to be able to share, through my photography, the many treasures I have found within our state. From my first book in 1981 through recent books and calendars, I continue to seek and uncover new troves of New Jersey's visual treasures.

In April of 1524, explorer Giovanni da Verrazano was probably the first European to navigate New Jersey's waters. Sailing for France aboard the ship "La Dauphine" he described the shore in a letter to the queen: "We followed a coast very green with forests ...and with some charming promontories and small rivers."

Eighty-five years later, Henry Hudson's ship "Halve Maen" returned to the New Jersey shore exploring for the Dutch East India Company. On September 2, 1609, Robert Juet entered in the ship's log his first impressions of the state: "This is a very good land to fall in with - and a pleasant land to see."

New Jersey is a pleasant land indeed! Early explorers as well as most current residents and visitors agree. Even transferees, that feared the worst, are also pleasantly surprised.

The Lenape named this land Scheyichbi—loosely translated to mean "the land bordering the water," or sometimes translated as "the land of the shell wampum." Wampum was the highly valued purple spot inside the clam shell which was fashioned into beads and used as a form of money. Treasure!

The Atlantic Ocean borders Scheyichbi with 127 miles of white sand beaches. Its other waters include hundreds of miles of rivers, bays and coastal wetlands. During ancient times the ocean covered the southern half of the state. Today this region is now the Coastal Plain and features the pristine Pine Barrens and a fertile stretch of farmland famous for Jersey tomatoes, peaches and a variety of other produce.

Moving northwesterly from the coast, the land rises slightly with rolling hills and becomes the Piedmont region—home to New Jersey's cities and expanding suburban townships which unfortunately are replacing most of the original woodlands and farms. Piedmont means "at the foot of the mountains."

North of the Piedmont lies the Highlands region, sometimes referred to as New Jersey's "Skylands." These upland hills and small mountains contain a treasury of minerals and ores, and are still heavily forested and dotted with abundant lakes which were created during the Ice Age's last glaciation over 18,000 years ago.

The Appalachian Mountains, formed from continental collisions millions of years ago, run from Maine to Georgia, passing through New Jersey with one mountain, named Kittatinny, meaning "the endless mountain." Rising over 1800 feet above sea level, High Point offers lofty vistas of New Jersey, New York and Pennsylvania; and the majestic Delaware River passes beneath Mount Tammany through the spectacular Delaware Water Gap.

From the first Lenape settlements, through early colonization by the Dutch, Swedes and Finns—later by the English, Scots and Irish, and continuing for over 350 years with emigration from all corners of the world, New Jersey is now one of the most culturally and ethnically diverse states in America. Hundreds of ethnic groups are found within the state's 8.4 million inhabitants.

The Proprietors encouraged settlers to bring their African slaves and their indentured servants to develop the new colony, promising free acreage as an incentive. New Jersey's moral and social attitudes improved through the 18th and 19th centuries as some early abolitionists from the state were integral in the formation of the Underground Railroad.

The state's motto "Liberty and Prosperity" illustrates the freedom and opportunity found by many that came to New Jersey —rich and poor alike.   At the turn of the 20th century, thousands of immigrants seeking those gifts entered through Ellis Island, as did my ancestors who came from Poland and Slovakia —some settling in Perth Amboy before moving on to Pennsylvania.

Liberty does not come without a price and New Jersey was pivotal in the fight for America's independence.   Known as the "Crossroads of the Revolution," New Jersey is hallowed ground for five major battles and hundreds of other skirmishes.   Numerous "Washington's Headquarters" are found throughout the state as General Washington spent much of the Revolution and three winters in New Jersey.   General Washington's 1776 Crossing of the Delaware is reenacted each Christmas and is forever immortalized on New Jersey's state quarter.

Memorials commemorating New Jersey's part of more recent wars are found across the state, and America's most decorated battleship, U.S.S. New Jersey, has recently come home to Camden to be celebrated once again.

Prosperity is the outcome of freedom, opportunity and invention. Some of New Jersey's renowned inventors include Edison, Marconi and Einstein, along with innumerable others who helped fuel America's industrial revolution.   New Jersey's rich industrial past has been transformed into a high-tech and information economy.

Positioned at the heart of the northeast corridor New Jersey has always been a hub and vanguard for all modes of transport.   Indian trails became roads, highways and turnpikes; seaports, rivers and canals preceded modern rail and air pathways. The first balloon flight in America landed in Gloucester County, in 1793, and today Newark International Airport is the country's busiest in the northeast.

I continue to journey those same roads and pathways traveled by many that have come before me. I appreciate and enjoy the many treasures I find— both natural and man-made, yet I'm always looking for something new.

New Netherlands, New Sweden, Nova Caesaria, ...New Jersey!

10. *Ellis Island,*
Jersey City

11. *Frankford,*
Sussex County

12. *Great Auditorium,*
Ocean Grove

13. *Mullica River,*
Green Bank

14. *Jenkinson's Boardwalk, Point Pleasant Beach*   15. *Casino Pier, Seaside Heights*

16. *Mercer Portico,*
Princeton Battlefield
State Park, Princeton

17. *Dvoor Farm,*
Flemington

18. *First United Methodist Church,*
Cape May Court House

19. *Space Farms Zoo and Museum,*
Beemerville

20. *Lenni-Lenape statue,*
Atlantic County Court House,
Mays Landing

21. *Nanticoke Lenni-Lenape Annual Pow-Wow, Sharptown*

22. *The Rutgers Gardens, New Brunswick*

23. *Roosevelt Park, Edison*

24. *Bridgeton City Park, Bridgeton*

25. *Cape May*
Fire Department Museum,
Cape May

26. *Edison Laboratory,*
Edison National Historic Site,
West Orange

27. *Glenmont Estate,*
Llewellyn Park
Edison National Historic Site,
West Orange

28. *Northampton Street Bridge, Phillipsburg*

29. *State House,*
Trenton

30. *French Garden,*
The Gardens at
Duke Farms,
Hillsborough

31. *Craftsman Farms,
The Gustav
Stickley Museum,
Parsippany*

32. *Nest of rabbits,*
South Branch

33. *Mount Tammany,*
Delaware Water Gap

34. *Hancock House,*
Hancocks Bridge

35. *Great Swamp,*
Meyersville

36. *Allentown Lake, Allentown*   37. *Princeton University Band, Princeton*

38. *Amusements, Wildwood*

39. *Under the boardwalk, Atlantic City*

Overleaf
40-41. *Newark and westerly view*

42. *Hamburg Mountain Wildlife*
Management Area, Hardyston

43. *Delaware Presbyterian Church,*
Knowlton Township

44. *Hamilton House, Clifton*   45. *Eagle Rock Reservation, Essex County*

46. Antiques shop,
Chester

47. Auction,
Cape May

48. *Vernon Summit, Mountain Creek Resort, Vernon*　　　49. *Ringwood Manor State Park, Ringwood*

50. *Herb garden,*
Ryland Inn,
Whitehouse

51. *Ann Whitall House,*
Red Bank Battlefield Park, National Park

52. *Minuteman statue, Springfield*

53. *Battleship U.S.S. New Jersey, Camden*

54. *Basking Ridge Oak, Basking Ridge*

55. *The Steuben House, River Edge*

56. *Statue of Justice,
Somerset County
Court House,
Somerville*

57. Statue of Mercury,
Post Office,
Burlington City

58. *Farmstand, Culver Lake*

59. *Lake Mohawk, Sparta*

60. *Sundew,*
Penn State Forest

61. *Gladstone Driving Event, Gladstone*

62. *Presby Memorial Iris Gardens,*
Upper Montclair

63. *Barnegat Lighthouse,*
Barnegat Light

64. *Marina District, Atlantic City*   65. *Outerbridge Crossing, Perth Amboy*

66. *Oyster boat, Maurice River*   67. *East Point Lighthouse, Heislerville*

68. *Nassau Presbyterian Church, Princeton*   69. *Nassau Hall, Princeton*

70. *Jacob Ford Mansion,*
Morristown National Historic Park, Morristown

71. *Wick House and Farm, Jockey Hollow,*
Morristown National Historic Park, Morristown

Overleaf
72-73. *Red Mill Museum Village, Clinton*

74. Karen's
At Brookside,
Hopewell

75. *Festival,*
Ironbound section,
Newark

76. *Snow Geese, Edwin B. Forsythe National Wildlife Refuge, Brigantine*   77. *Cape May "Diamonds," Cape May Point*

78. *Crosswicks Library,*
Crosswicks

79. Miller-Cory House, Westfield

80. *St. Stephen Episcopal Church, Mullica Hill*   81. *Washington Spring Garden, Van Saun Park, Paramus*

82. *Sunrise Mountain,*
Stokes State Forest

83. *Millbrook Village,*
Delaware Water Gap National Recreation Area

84. *Surfers, Manasquan*   85. *Great Adventure, Jackson*

86. *Morven,*
Princeton

87. Essex Fox Hounds,
Peapack

88. *State Botanical Garden at Skylands, Ringwood*

89. *Dey Mansion,*
Wayne

90. *George Washington Bridge, Fort Lee*

91. *Railroad bridge, New Brunswick*

92. *South Shore Marina, Greenwood Lake, Hewitt*

93. *American Labor Museum, Haledon*

94. *Kingston Flour Mill, Kingston*   95. *Whitesbog, Lebanon State Forest*

96. *Wortendyke Barn,*
Park Ridge

97. *Great Falls,*
Paterson

98. Branch Brook Park,
Belleville

99. *Columbia Avenue,*
Cape May

100. *Turtle,*
Hacklebarney State Park

101. *Pennypacker Park,*
Haddonfield

102. *Horse Park of New Jersey, Stone Tavern, Monmouth County*

103. *Horse Farm, Bedminster*

Overleaf
104-105. *Fosterfields Living Historical Farm, Morristown*

106. *Old Tennent Presbyterian Church, Tennent*

107. *Salem Oak, Friends Burial Ground, Salem*

108. *Peaches, Turnersville*

109. *Farm field, Greenwich*

110. *Port Elizabeth, Elizabeth*

111. *Kill Van Kull and Bayonne Bridge, Bayonne*

112. *Newark International Airport, Newark*   113. *Pulaski Skyway, Hackensack River*

114. *Independence Day fireworks, Lake Hopatcong*

115. *New Jersey Festival of Ballooning, Readington*

116. *The Proprietary House,*
Perth Amboy

117. *Surveyor General's Office,*
Burlington City

118. *Molly Pitcher Marina, Red Bank*   119. *Sandy Hook, Monmouth County*

120. *Liberty State Park,*
Jersey City

121: *Nelson House, Washington Crossing State Park, Titusville*

122. *Island Beach*
State Park,
Ocean County

123. *New Jersey
State Aquarium,
Camden*

124. *Mannington Meadow, Salem County*

125. *Rahway River, Cranford*

126. *Washington Street, Hoboken*

127. *Cranberry harvest, Chatsworth*

Overleaf
128. *Cape May Lighthouse, Cape May Point*